The Truth Seeker's Library™

Health Is One Of God's Great Blessings!

Roger Henri Trepanier

© 2016

This book is dedicated to all the men and women of this world who realize that our bodies belong to God and that we are only stewards of them for Him!

"Bless the Lord, O my soul, and forget none of His benefits… Who heals all your diseases…"

Psalm 103:2,3 in part

**Titles available from Roger Henri Trepanier in
The Truth Seeker's Library™ series:**

God Did Not Create Human Beings To Die... But To Live
On... Eternally!
Finding Comfort And Encouragement In The Promises Of God
In The Last Days
How We Know For Sure That We Are Living In The Last Days!
Have You Ever Wondered What Happens After Death?
An Introduction To The New World That Is Coming On The
Earth
Deeper Truths Of The Christian Life
Evangelism As God Intended
Keeping On Serving God In The Last Days
The Mysterious World Of Angels And Demons
No One Loves As He Loves!
Thanks Be To God For His Indescribable Gift!
The Church Is Very Much Alive, Well, And Growing!
Tracing The Steps Of The Son Of God From Eternity To
Eternity!
War, And Going To War, Is Simply Not Of God!
God Never Meant Prayer To Be A Mystery!

**Titles available from Roger Henri Trepanier in
The Practical Helps Library™ series:**

Learning to Overcome The Perplexities Of This Present Life
So, I Hear You Want To Work With Seniors?
I Will Not Have This Man To Rule Over Me!
Spiritual Truth To Warm The Heart!
Fasten Your Seatbelts: Turbulence Ahead!
Living A Normal Christian Life In An Increasingly Abnormal
World!

**Titles available from Roger Henri Trepanier
in The Christian Fiction Library™ series:**

The Beginning Of A New Dawn
It Is Never Too Late For Love!
The True To Life Musings Of Fred And Ernie
Between A Rock And A Hard Place!

Love Knows No Boundaries!
A Woman Worth Pursuing!

**Titles available from Roger Henri Trepanier
in The Word Of God Library™ series:**

God's First Letter To The Thessalonians
God's Second Letter To The Thessalonians

INTRODUCTION

The older we get, the more we realize just how precious health is! When we are young, meaning still in our teens and our twenties, we think that our bodies are made of titanium and will last forever in their present condition! When we were that age, we thought that we could drink and eat anything and we certainly had no concern for our health, unless we were born with a health condition, which was true of few of us. What generally makes us think of our health for the first time is when a woman is expecting her first child; or for the rest of us, when we experience that first major health issue that threatens our lives.

And although health is indeed precious, this is not a book on health per se. That is, this book will not deal with specific health conditions in terms of offering remedies. For one thing, I am not a health professional, but rather an evangelist. My area of expertise is the spiritual, not the physical. So why write a book on health, then? Simply because God, Who is after all The One Who designed us and then created us, knows more about health than the entire human race combined. Since He wrote the manual for what works and what does not relating to our health, then we would be foolish indeed to not pay attention to what He has to say! At least I believe so.

One of the truths we will come to see from reading the book is that our bodies really belong to God and we are but stewards of them for Him. A few years ago, the family doctor I was going to at the time had a sign on his wall, which one could not miss in coming into his office. It read, "Your health is your responsibility. I am only here to help you achieve it." The first time I read that, I thought that doctor had the right idea. God does not just give us physical life on this earth and then goes away to leave us to our own devices. On the contrary, He is there each moment of every day throughout our existence here on earth at the ready to help us achieve maximum health. But He too holds us responsible for the way we live, which in turn will impact our overall health. And of course that includes our spiritual health as well, which is even more important, since it eventually determines our eternal destiny!

Therefore, this book looks at health from God's perspective, that is, based on the manual that He wrote to guide human beings during our time on this earth. And as is true on all subjects relating to God's manual, no subject is ever dealt with in one place. In other words, God has been speaking about health since He placed the first man and woman on this earth, and then continued to speak about it until the end of the first century AD, which is when His manual was completed. What this means then is the most of the background for this book comes from a study of God's manual which took almost three months to complete, where words such as sickness and disease were looked up, for it is in knowing what God says about what ails us that we can maintain good health.

What should also be mentioned, as we bring this Introduction to a close, is that after completing twenty-one years of formal education and then spending almost twenty-eight years working in Project Engineering and Management in the Corporate offices of a large utility, God called His servant as a non-denominational evangelist in early 1999, and then sent him out over 2500 miles, away from family and friends, to the place of service God assigned, which is where His servant has been and is still serving Him as evangelist, counselor, author, editor, and publisher. The author is a widower with three adopted children, all now married.

It has also been my great pleasure to write, under God's guiding Hand, nine Commentaries of books of the Bible, with some of these Commentaries taking from 3 to 4 years to complete. Also, there have been over 535 Devotional Commentaries on portions of the Bible, including more than 100 studies on various subjects found in the Bible. The foregoing work has been the foundation material that God has used in His servant's counseling ministry these last 20 plus years, and also the background information to have in giving the sermon in as part of a local church for 52 Sundays over a period of four years. And now God is using a lot of this material as background material for the writing of these books. All of this is to the glory of God alone, for the author knows full well that apart from God's grace and power, he cannot do anything that will last for time and eternity!

A website has been established for the purpose of interacting with readers, which can be found at:

http://www.pilgrimpathwaypublications.com

God had also led His servant to establish another website specifically for gospel ministry, since the author is an evangelist. That website can be found at:

http://servantofmosthigh.com

And now my prayer is that God will richly bless you as you read this book, and greatly minister to your every need in your life, as only God can! To Him be all praise, honor, and glory, with thanksgiving, for both time and for all eternity!

CONTENTS

"God saw all that He had made, and behold, it was very good. And there was evening and there was morning, the sixth day."

Genesis 1:31

CHAPTER ONE

/ Mankind was in perfect health when first created by God!

When God finished with creation at the end of six literal days, He looked upon it all, which included human beings, and exclaimed, "...behold, it was very good" (Genesis 1:31). And since whatever God does cannot ever be improved upon, then we can be sure that God's "very good" was 'beyond awesome to the nth degree!' What this means, of course, is that our first set of parents, Adam and Eve, enjoyed perfect health, free of all disease and sickness, since as God's first pair from whom we are all derived, they were made in the very image of God (Genesis 1:26), Who is in His Persons the epitome of perfection, including health!

The obvious question becomes then: Why do we see so many unhealthy human beings, in general, with so much disease, sickness, and death, abounding everywhere we look? And the answer is a little three letter word, which has spawned all the misery in the world since it was introduced into the human race, that being SIN! During the three and half year ministry of God's Son on earth, The Lord Jesus Christ, He was recorded as making the following comment to a man whom he had just healed of a sickness he had been afflicted with for 38 years, "Behold, you have become well; DO NOT SIN ANYMORE, SO THAT NOTHING WORSE HAPPENS TO YOU" (John 5:14).

This is the kind of statement that makes one sit up and take notice, for it expresses a truth that is usually not apparent to us, in that we do not generally connect human disease and sickness with sin. But the awful reality is that all disease and sickness on earth indeed have their existence due to the entrance of sin into the human condition! And we would benefit here in examining four of these proofs that this is so.

Proof number one is that before sin entered God's perfect original creation, there was no disease or sickness anywhere on earth, only perfect health! These only came after sin entered the human race. And if we look at the other end of the continuum, when time, which began with God's creation (Genesis 1:14), ends again to begin the eternal state without the measurement of time, there will be no disease or sickness on God's new earth, only perfect health again, since there will not be any sin there, noting what God tells us about this at Revelation 21:1,3,4, "[1] Then I saw a new heaven and a new earth; for the first heaven and the first earth passed away (of the original creation of God), and there is no longer any sea... [3] And I heard a loud voice from the throne, saying, "Behold, the tabernacle of God is among men, and He will dwell among them, and they shall be His people, and God Himself will be among them, [4] and He will wipe away every tear from their eyes; and there will no longer be any death; there will no longer be any mourning, or crying, or pain; the first things (relating to the original creation) have passed away."

And here is a second proof that disease and sickness have their basis in sin. All of these conditions can lead, and often do lead, to death, which is a direct result of the presence of sin in the human condition, noting what God tells us in His manual at Romans 5:12, where He makes that connection, "Therefore, just as through one man (Adam) sin entered into the world, and death through sin, and so death spread to all men, because all sinned." When a human being eventually dies, it is usually due to some disease or sickness, which has affected one's body. And there would be no death had there not been any sin, as God says in His manual at Romans 6:23 in part, "For the wages of sin is death..."

We can be thankful for one thing, as human beings, which is that God never leaves us without remedy, in that He always provides a way for us to escape the consequences of sin. And so here in that statement we are to see a very important third and fourth proof that disease and sickness have their basis in sin, for the third proof is that when God's own Son, The Lord Jesus Christ, was on earth at His first coming, He was sinless, and as a result He was free of disease and sickness during the thirty-three and a half years He was on earth! In other words, He was a perfect specimen of health, same as the first man Adam had been before sin entered God's original creation.

And the fourth proof is that at the end of His thirty-three and a half years on earth neared, in the will of God His Father, He willingly went to the cross to bear the sins of the whole human race, so that God His Father would then have a basis to forgive the sins of any who believe in His work on our behalf. But that is not all, here is what God says at Romans 8:16,17 regarding our diseases and sicknesses as a result of God's Son bearing the sins of the human race at the cross, "[16] When evening came, they brought to Him (God's Son, The Lord Jesus Christ) many who were demon-possessed; and He cast out the spirits with a word, and HEALED ALL WHO WERE ILL. [17] This was to fulfill what was spoken through Isaiah the prophet (Isaiah 53:4): "HE HIMSELF TOOK OUR INFIRMITIES (in reference to our sicknesses and ailments) AND CARRIED AWAY OUR DISEASES."

What this means then, relating to our fourth proof, is that faith in God's Son brings the forgiveness of our sins, which then makes healing from God possible for our diseases and sicknesses! In other words, God made provision for our being healthy as human beings in the death of God's Son at the cross, because it was there that our sins were dealt with, and in dealing with sin in the death of His Son, God made it possible for human beings to not only be forgiven of their sins by God, but also to be delivered from disease and sickness, which are due to sin!

This further means that in one becoming a believer in The Lord Jesus Christ, which further means that one is now a child of God and part of the family of God, one's sins have been forgiven and one is being imparted God's righteous life, that is,

17

righteousness to live by. And in cleansing us of our sins at salvation, God also works to free us, who are His children, of all disease and sickness! That this is so can be discerned from what God tells believers at Psalm 103:2,3, "[2] Bless the Lord, O my soul, and forget none of His benefits; [3] Who pardons all your iniquities, Who heals all your diseases..." Since God says it, we can count on it that it is true! And of course over the years believers have believed it and have acted upon that truth, noting what one such believer said to God at Psalm 30:2, "O Lord my God, I cried to You for help, and You healed me."

As we conclude this very important first chapter then, we see clearly that when first created by God, human beings were in perfect health. It was the entrance of sin into God's perfect original creation which brought disease and sickness, leading to eventual death. But thankfully, through God's intervention, He provided a remedy for the forgiveness of our sins through the death of His own Son to pay the penalty due our sins, so that those who believe in Him can receive not only the forgiveness of sins, but also be delivered from any disease or sickness!

"Beloved, I pray that in all respects you may prosper and be in good health, just as your soul prospers."

3 John 1:2

CHAPTER TWO

/ God makes it clear that one's physical health is dependent upon one's spiritual health!

What we need to do in this chapter is to establish a spiritual foundation, which God wants each of His children to have after salvation and as long as we are on earth, in order to be able to enjoy as much health as is possible. What we mention here is apart from the fact that our present world is getting more and polluted by the day and the food we eat is far less nutritious than in our parent's day, due to the continual depletion of the essential elements in the soil, which cannot help but have a drastic effect in general upon our health. We will discuss such things in more detail in a later chapter, but for now let us be aware first of all that our spiritual condition as human beings does indeed affect our physical health!

1) God's healing of His own begins with one's salvation!

It is very important that we be aware that God's healing is only for those who become His children through salvation, so that in forgiving us of our sins, due to His Son having already died at the cross to provide us that forgiveness, God not only renders us well spiritually, but also begins the healing of our lives physically, since sin is at the root of all disease and sickness, and we have just had our sins forgiven by God at the moment of our salvation! So how critical then, that after salvation, we ensure that we go on living each day with no known unconfessed sins in our lives. This then is the foundation for our being healthy, that we continually be free of any known unconfessed sins in our lives!

And to ensure that we are all on the same page here, it would be beneficial for us to briefly review what happens at the beginning of our salvation, at the moment that God saved our souls, with there being two important events which occurred at that point. As we believed the gospel, which is the good news of what God's Son did on our behalf in His death for our sins, His burial, and His subsequent resurrection from the dead the third day, God The Father gave us His Holy Spirit to indwell our human spirits. And as The Holy Spirit came to indwell us, all the sins we committed against God since our infancy were cleansed away by God, while at the same time God imparted to us His own eternal and righteous life, or righteousness, to live by.

One of the critical truths to know and remember here is that this eternal life is the very life that God Himself ever lives, and which His Son ever lived while on earth. In other words, this life is the only life that God is ever pleased with! And this is the life that God wants to continue to impart to us after our having initially received it from Him through His Son by The Holy Spirit at salvation. And relating to our present subject, we are now to realize that God imparted us His life initially because we had just been cleansed of all our sins to begin our new life with Him. And so the condition for our continuing to receive God's life for us to live by after our initial moment of salvation is simply to ensure that we remain with NO KNOWN UNCONFESSED SINS IN OUR LIVES!

In case there are any readers who would like to know where God teaches us about what has been shared here, the answer is that one key verse is 1 John 1:9, where God says, "If we confess our sins, He is faithful and righteous to forgive us our sins and to cleanse us from all unrighteousness," and which I call 'the believer's only confessional provided by God;' while the other key passage is what God says to us at Romans 8:9-11, with comments being added in brackets to further help us, "[9] However, you are not in the flesh but in the (Holy) Spirit, if indeed the (Holy) Spirit of God dwells in you. But if anyone does not have the Spirit of Christ, he does not belong to Him. [10] If Christ is in you (spiritually speaking, by The Holy Spirit's indwelling us), though the body is dead because of sin (speaking of our nature which is sinful in God's sight), yet the spirit (human) is alive because of righteousness (which is God's imparted life, being the "life" He gives us of verse 11). [11] But if the (Holy) Spirit of Him (God The Father) who raised Jesus from the dead dwells in you, He (God The Father) who raised Christ Jesus from the dead will also give life (His own life, which enables us to live righteously on earth, in a way which pleases Him) to your mortal bodies through His (Holy) Spirit who dwells in you."

In God's sight, our spiritual life with Him comes first and is of paramount importance, as it affects the physical life that we also have with Him, which is every breath we draw. Each of these is a gift from God! Therefore, how important that we be aware that if we want to be healthy physically, then we first need to ensure that we are well spiritually with God. There are two passages which we can note here to further bring this truth to our hearts and minds, the first being at Romans 14:17,18, where God tells us, "[17] for the kingdom of God is not eating and drinking, but righteousness and peace and joy in the Holy Spirit. [18] For he who in this way serves Christ is acceptable to God and approved by men."

And the second passage is at 1 Corinthians 6:13,19,20 where God tells us, "]13] Food is for the stomach and the stomach is for food, but God will do away with both of them. Yet the body is not for immorality, but for the Lord, and the Lord is for the body... [19] Or do you not know that your body is a temple of the Holy Spirit who is in you, whom you have from God, and that you are not your own? [20] For you have been bought with a price: therefore glorify God in your body." As we see from these passages, our physical bodies are primarily for serving God, which is spiritual, rather than merely the physical, which is secondary.

2) God makes it very clear from His word that only believers are subject to His healing, since unbelievers are under His wrath due to yet being in unbelief

We need to also be aware that God's healing not only begins at salvation, as we have just seen above, but that God's healing is only for believers, as those who are part of His family by new spiritual birth; while unbelievers are under His wrath and subject to His judgment due to yet being in their sins. In other words, unbelievers have never believed in God's Son in order to have their sins forgiven by God, as we have, and since unforgiven sin is at the root of disease and sickness, this therefore means that unbelievers are not protected by God from all the disease and sickness in the world due to sin!

And now we will look at some passages of God's word to see where God makes this very clear to us, noting for instance what God says at Exodus 15:26, "And He (God) said, "If you will give earnest heed to the voice of the Lord your God, and do what is right in His sight, and give ear to His commandments, and keep all His statutes, I WILL PUT NONE OF THE DISEASES ON YOU WHICH I HAVE PUT on the Egyptians (representing unbelievers); FOR I, THE LORD, AM YOUR HEALER (speaking in regards to believers)." We clearly see here that one's spiritual condition vis-a-vis God determines one's physical condition in this world, in terms of being free from disease and sickness!

Later on at Deuteronomy 28, God elaborated on this, for there, after God gave a long list to the nation of Israel of the blessings of obedience to His word; He followed that with a long list of the consequences due to one's sin, which we are to see are always against Him (Psalm 51:4), noting what God there said at verses 58 to 61, "[58] If you are not careful to observe all the words of this law which are written in this book, to fear this honored and awesome name, the Lord your God, [59] then the Lord will bring extraordinary plagues on you and your descendants, even severe and lasting plagues, and miserable and chronic sicknesses. [60] He will bring back on you all the diseases of Egypt of which you were afraid, and they will cling to you. [61] Also every sickness and every plague which, not written in the book of this law, the Lord will bring on you until you are destroyed (that is, until you die)."

So let us remember that living as pleasing to God, which God makes known is by being free of any known unconfessed sins in our lives so as to be imparted God's own life to live by, is

24

the one condition for one being healed of one's diseases and sicknesses, and for not being under the judgment of God as unbelievers are, noting what God says to unbelievers at John 3:18,36 in regards to this, "[18] He who believes in Him is not judged; he who does not believe has been judged already, because he has not believed in the name of the only begotten Son of God... [36] He who believes in the Son has eternal life; but he who does not obey the Son will not see life, but the wrath of God abides on him." Again, unbelievers are unforgiven human beings, and since still living in their sins, which is the root of every disease and sickness, then they are not under God's protection from such as believers are, but rather yet subject to His wrath!

We also need to ever remember that the sin of human beings cost God the physical life of His Son; as we have seen. And God also made provision for the healing of disease and sickness in the death of His Son. Therefore, when unbelievers choose to remain in unbelief, then they are choosing to remain subject to disease and sickness! Let us further notice here what God says to unbelievers at Jeremiah 30:12-15 in part, "[12] For thus says the Lord, 'Your wound is incurable and your injury is serious. [13] There is no one to plead your cause; no healing for your sore, no recovery for you. [14] ...For I have wounded you with the wound of an enemy, with the punishment of a cruel one, because your iniquity is great and your sins are numerous. [15] Why do you cry out over your injury? Your pain is incurable. Because your iniquity is great and your sins are numerous, I have done these things to you."

But someone might say here: 'But I know many unbelievers who are in good health; they do not appear to have any disease or be sick more often than others.' Let us note a few things in regards to such a statement. First, here is what God says to unbelievers at Romans 2:4 regarding what He is like, "Or do you think lightly of the riches of His kindness and tolerance and patience, not knowing that the kindness of God leads you to repentance?" And here is what we further read of what God is like at Nahum 1:3a, "The Lord is slow to anger and great in power, and the Lord will by no means leave the guilty unpunished," and also noting what God says regarding ALL unbelievers at Isaiah 48:22, ""There is no peace for the wicked (that is, unbelievers)," says the Lord." In other words, we may only be observing these persons occasionally, not walking in their shoes from day to day. As we have just read, unbelievers may be shown patience by God as He waits for these to repent and turn to Him in salvation, but until they do, they have no peace and are still under the judgment of God, which can show itself in disease and sickness at any moment!

Another truth to keep in mind is that not all unbelievers will remain unbelievers until physical death, and so be separated from God forever; in that some unbelievers will come to know God in salvation at some point in their lives. After all, we were all unbelievers ourselves before coming to know God in salvation! Let us note what God says at 1 Corinthians 6:9-11 in this regard, "[9] Or do you not know that the unrighteous will not inherit the kingdom of God? Do not be deceived; neither fornicators, nor idolaters, nor adulterers, nor effeminate, nor homosexuals, [10] nor thieves, nor the covetous, nor drunkards, nor revilers, nor swindlers, will inherit the kingdom of God. [11] SUCH WERE SOME OF YOU; but you were washed (forgiven of all sin), but you were sanctified (set apart for God's service only), but you were justified (imparted God's righteousness) in the name of the Lord Jesus Christ and in the Spirit of our God." Now we can answer the statement made above from our own life situation, in the sense of how many of us while yet unbelievers were disease free and sickness free? Most likely none!

Let me also illustrate the above truth by saying that I have had a ministry among seniors for the last twenty-six years, and in that time, God did save many of these seniors, some while in their seventies, others in their eighties and beyond, as God did save one man of 102! Now all of these, apart from the man of 102, were in a care facility due to a stroke. I think the older man was there due to no longer being able to care for himself. The fact is that God did keep them alive because He knew that one day these would become His, and obviously gave them a measure of health for them to reach that wonderful day, but not entirely, as they had almost all had suffered a stroke. I knew at least one who had a nervous breakdown and had her kids placed in an orphanage after her husband left her; and another who had been married three times; another who was an alcoholic, and so forth. All had less than ideal life situations and health, at least nothing any of us would have desired to have! In other words, the life of unbelievers only appears to be pleasant while they are still in their unforgiven sins!

There is yet another truth relating to unbelievers, which we need to note here, which God shares with us at Romans 9:22-24 in part, "[22] What if God, although willing to demonstrate His wrath and to make His power known, endured with much patience vessels of wrath prepared for destruction (that is, unbelievers)? [23] And He did so to make known the riches of His glory upon vessels of mercy (that is, believers), which He prepared beforehand for glory, [24] even us…" In other words, God endures unbelievers and allows them to live only to serve His purposes involuntarily; while God saved us as believers that we might come to know all the riches of God while serving Him voluntarily. Along the way, we might observe an unbeliever or two who seem to have it pretty good, but let us be assured that if that is the case, then it is only for a short time, and it is only because God is having mercy on their soul at that point in time, waiting on them to repent!

Let us close this chapter with an illustration of this truth from an example from God's word. It is found at Psalm 73 and concerns what God had a believer write down regarding unbelievers, as one who was thinking at first that they seemed to have it fairly good on earth when contrasted to believers, since it is never easy for believers to live anywhere on earth in the midst of so many unbelievers, noting first what we read at verse 2 to 5, "[2] But as for me, my feet came close to stumbling, my steps had almost slipped. [3] For I was envious of the arrogant as I saw the prosperity of the wicked. [4] For there are no pains in their death, and their body is fat. [5] They are not in trouble as other men, nor are they plagued like mankind."

But then let us notice what this believer was next led to say, once God had led him to see these unbelievers in a truer light, noting what we now read at verses 16 to 19, "[16] When I pondered to understand this, it was troublesome in my sight [17] Until I came into the sanctuary of God; then I perceived their end. [18] Surely You set them in slippery places; You cast them down to destruction. 19] How they are destroyed in a moment! They are utterly swept away by sudden terrors!"

So let us remember that unbelievers are on a slippery slope on their way to an eternal hell, even though momentarily here and there in time they appear to have it good. Yet the reality is that they are still on that slippery slope, unless God intervenes in salvation! So the truth to remember from this chapter is that God's healing from disease and sickness can only start once one becomes a child of God at salvation and until then unbelievers are under the wrath and judgment of God, subject to all the diseases and sickness found in the world!

"There is no soundness in my flesh because of Your indignation; there is no health in my bones because of my sin."

Psalm 38:3

CHAPTER THREE

/ Realizing that disease or sickness in a believer's life may not always be due to sin!

A question which may have entered the mind of one reading this book, who as a believer may at the moment have some sickness or disease, is: Does this mean that my disease or sickness is due to some sin in my life now, or which I have committed in the past? Before we go on to provide an answer to this question under the following headings, we need to remember two truths here; the first being that disease and sickness is never a coincidence or a chance occurrence, but is always something as allowed of God to serve some purpose of His, this being true in regards to both believers and unbelievers. What this also means then is that health is totally under God's control, as is of course true in regards to all things in existence that may affect human beings, such as conception and death itself! And the second truth to remember as we go on is that not all disease and sickness which may come to a believer is due to known unconfessed sins in one's life!

1) Sometimes a physical condition, disease or sickness may be allowed of God as a way to bring Him glory in demonstrating His power!

To begin with, we need to see that God sometimes allows some physical condition, disease or sickness in order to bring glory to Himself in the demonstration of His unlimited power! We will give two examples from God's word here to reinforce this truth. The first is found in what God tells us at John 9:1-3,

"[1] As He passed by, He saw a man blind from birth. [2] And His disciples asked Him, "Rabbi (that is, 'Teacher'), who sinned, this man or his parents, that he would be born blind?" [3] Jesus answered, "It was neither that this man sinned, nor his parents; but it was so that the works of God might be displayed in him." And so, as we see in this first example, neither the man sinned, nor his parents, for him to have been born blind, but rather, this had been allowed of God so that when His Son came to earth, He might give this man's sight back to him as a display of God's miracle-working power!

Now let us look at a second example from God's word, this time noting what God tells us at John 11:1,3-6, "[1] Now a certain man was sick, Lazarus of Bethany, the village of Mary and her sister Martha... [3] So the sisters sent word to Him, saying, "Lord, behold, he whom You love is sick." [4] But when Jesus heard this, He said, "This sickness is not to end in death, but for the glory of God, so that the Son of God may be glorified by it." [5] Now Jesus loved Martha and her sister and Lazarus. [6] So when He heard that he was sick, He then stayed two days longer in the place where He was." In other words, He waited until Lazarus has died before returning to Bethany.

Again, we are to observe that Lazarus' sickness was not due to some sin he had committed, but rather was allowed of God so that it would result in his death, which then gave God's Son on earth an opportunity to glorify His Father in Heaven by raising him from the dead again, to show that God had the miracle-working power to do so, noting what we read further on in this same chapter at John 11:38-45, [38] So Jesus, again being deeply moved within, came to the tomb. Now it was a cave, and a stone was lying against it. [39] Jesus said, "Remove the stone." Martha, the sister of the deceased, said to Him, "Lord, by this time there will be a stench, for he has been dead four days." [40] Jesus said to her, "Did I not say to you that if you believe, you will see the glory of God?" [41] So they removed the stone. Then Jesus raised His eyes, and said, "Father, I thank You that You have heard Me. [42] I knew that You always hear Me; but because of the people standing around I said it, so that they may believe that You sent Me."

[43] When He had said these things, He cried out with a loud voice, "Lazarus, come forth." [44] The man who had died came forth, bound hand and foot with wrappings, and his face was wrapped around with a cloth. Jesus said to them, "Unbind him, and let him go." [45] Therefore many of the Jews who came to Mary, and saw what He had done, believed in Him."

And before going to the next section, let us consider one example from my own past experience. I had been a believer for about ten years when this occurred. In the local church that my wife and I were part of at the time, there was a Christian lady attending there through whom God worked to bring many of the children to a saving knowledge of Himself, who passed through her Sunday School class. At the time I was on the church board and when one board member suggested that she be made Sunday School Superintendent, I objected, saying that we needed to keep her in her present position for the sake of the building up of the Kingdom of God, since being the Superintendent would have meant that she would no longer have her Sunday School class.

In any case, a few months later, this woman fell ill, and was so ill that her doctor had her admitted to the hospital. I went to visit her while she was there and she said that even though the doctors were running all kinds of tests on her, they were unable to find out why she was so sick. However, we soon found out why she was sick, and in God's will, had been admitted to the hospital.

While she was there, a young mother was admitted to the bed next to hers. Within a few days, that young woman had come to know God. And as soon as she had become a believer, the woman who led her to faith in God was immediately well again, and was discharged from the hospital. About ten days later, the new believer was in our local fellowship on a Sunday morning, giving testimony to everyone she talked with of the fact that she had come to know God through the other woman while in the hospital. God gave His servant a wonderful display of His Sovereign working that day. And of course, it is one more example from everyday life of the fact that not all disease or illness in the life of a believer is due to sin!

2) Even believers are not immune from the consequences of known unconfessed sin in one's life, which sometimes is disease, sickness, and even death!

At the same time, we also need to ever keep in mind that believers still have a sinful nature, and will continue to have until the time of glorification, that is, until God's Son returns for us, at which point that sinful nature will be removed from us as we enter God's Presence to ever be with Him (1 Thessalonians 4:16,17). What this means then is that believers can still sin after salvation, and indeed do, which sometimes has an unwanted consequence. Let us note to begin with what God says in His word at Hebrews 13:4, "Marriage is to be held in honor among all (believers and unbelievers alike), and the marriage bed is to be undefiled; for fornicators and adulterers God will judge." Let us note God's words here - He will judge adulterers and fornicators, not that He might judge!

And please note that believers are not exempt from this. I know because I have personally counseled two believers over the years who had committed adultery in a moment of temptation; one being a man and the other a woman. In both cases, these believers got cancer and died, both being still in their early fifties. Now this does not mean that all believers who commit adultery will die of cancer, for God gives us the example of David at 2 Samuel 11:1-27, who not only committed adultery with Bathsheba, another man's wife, but he even had the woman's husband killed in order to cover up the fact that the woman had now become pregnant due to his sin. But as we see in the next chapter, at 2 Samuel 12:1-15, God did forgive David, but there was a consequence to his sin, for not only did the child Bathsheba was carrying die, but David had problems in his family for the rest of his life, which were a direct consequence of his sins relating to Bathsheba and her husband.

Let us take another example of a warning God gives believers regarding the consequences of sin, this time noting what God tells us at 1 Corinthians 11:26-31, "[26] For as often as you eat this bread and drink the cup, you proclaim the Lord's death

34

until He comes. [27] Therefore whoever eats the bread or drinks the cup of the Lord in an unworthy manner, shall be guilty of the body and the blood of the Lord. [28] But a man must examine himself, and in so doing he is to eat of the bread and drink of the cup. [29] For he who eats and drinks, eats and drinks judgment to himself if he does not judge the body rightly. [30] For this reason many among you are weak and sick, and a number sleep. [31] But if we judged ourselves rightly, we would not be judged."

Here we have the judgment of God relating to any believer who partakes of The Lord's Supper (communion) with known unconfessed sins in one's life. Since God's Son died in our place in order for God to have a basis to forgive us our sins, this then makes it grievous in God's sight when a believer partakes of The Lord's Supper, which brings that event to mind, while one has known unconfessed sins in one's life! So, because one was unwilling to come to God to have those sins forgiven before partaking, noting 1 John 1:9, which is the believer's only confessional after salvation, then God will judge that believer, if one partakes The Lord's Supper in such an unworthy manner!

And that is why God says at verse 30, "For this reason many among you are weak and sick, and a number sleep." In other words, as a result, that is why many are sick and even die, because they incurred the judgment of God for failing to judge themselves. The word "weak" here means 'without strength,' that is, with much less than optimum health. So how much we need to take sin seriously after salvation, simply because God does; and since we now represent Him on earth, Who is sinless, then we also need to display the family likeness! If we intend to be as healthy as possible, then we will indeed take sin as seriously as God does as believers!

3) God may allow a believer to incur a disease or sickness as His way to bring His child home to Heaven!

Of course, we are all very much conscious of the fact, especially if one is quite advanced in age, that we all have bodies that are subject to decay and eventual death, unless God's Son returns from Heaven to earth for us before physical death should come (1 Thessalonians 4:16,17). So the reality is that even though we might live without known unconfessed sins in our lives, we still all face physical death, which God must bring about in one way or another. In other words, God rarely, if ever, brings a believer home to Heaven through death due to 'old age.' Usually, there is some disease or sickness that God allows to overtake a believer's body, which leads to physical death.

Let us take two examples from God's word here to see this truth, noting first of all what God tells us at Genesis 48:1,2 with Genesis 49:33 regarding the patriarch Jacob, "[48:1] Now it came about after these things that Joseph was told, "Behold, your father is sick." So he took his two sons Manasseh and Ephraim with him.[2] When it was told to Jacob, "Behold, your son Joseph has come to you," Israel collected his strength and sat up in the bed... [49:33] When Jacob finished charging his sons, he drew his feet into the bed and breathed his last, and was gathered to his people." As we see here, God took Jacob home through a sickness He allowed, and not because Jacob had any known unconfessed sins in his life, but rather because it was his time to go!

Then a second example from God's word is noting what He tells us at 2 Kings 13,14,20 in part, "[14] When Elisha became sick with the illness of which he was to die... [20] Elisha died, and they buried him." Now as a prophet of God, we can be sure that Elisha had not sinned here, when he fell sick and died, or else God would no doubt have let us know of that fact. It was simply Elisha's God-appointed time for him to die, and God used a sickness to bring that death about. So when our time of departure from this life comes, we simply cannot avoid it!

The best thing to do, if we incur a disease or sickness as a child of God is to come to God and ask Him why one has incurred what one has. Sometimes it may be due to the time of one's homegoing having arrived, in which case God will almost always let one know that, noting 2 Peter 1:14. And if it is not the time of one's homegoing having arrived, one can ask God if there are any known unconfessed sins in one's life.

If there are none, then one can certainly pray to God for healing, for it is one of God's great benefits to His own, as we have seen in the dedication verse at the beginning of the book, where God says to us at Psalm 103:2,3, "[2] Bless the Lord, O my soul, and forget none of His benefits; [3] Who pardons all your iniquities, who heals all your diseases…"

"Delight yourself in the Lord and He will give you the desires of your heart."

Psalm 37:4

CHAPTER FOUR

/ Looking at some of the promises which God gives believers when they are faced with a disease or with sickness!

In this chapter, we want to look at some of the promises which God has given to believers over time when faced with some health condition, which would not be due to some known unconfessed sin in one's life, and which would not be due to one's time of homegoing having arrived. We will not only be looking at examples from God's word here, but also at examples from my own life, relating to passages of Scripture that I have personally made use of over the years. The one promise we can begin with, and keep in mind as we proceed throughout this chapter, is what God says to every believer of time at Exodus 15:26 in part, "I, The Lord, am your healer." Those are precious words to bring to mind when anxiety over one's health would seek to overwhelm us!

But God not only encourages His own by letting us know that He is our Healer, but He also gives us evidence of that fact in having had His Son heal every disease and sickness imaginable while He was here on earth at His first coming, noting what God tells us of Him at Matthew 4:24, "The news about Him spread throughout all Syria; and they brought to Him all who were ill, those suffering with various diseases and pains, demoniacs, epileptics, paralytics; and He healed them." These too are golden words to the child of God facing some disease or sickness, just to know that God has the power to heal us, and has demonstrated it when His Son was on earth!

What may also happen at times is that God may give us a promise from His word regarding our health only at the time we need it. This is what happened to me a few years ago. Most readers will be aware that in September 2008, there was a financial meltdown of the global economy. This was a disastrous time for anyone living off their savings, as I was at the time. From when God called me as an evangelist in early 1999, I had been mostly supporting my ministry through my life-savings. What this meant was that any funds not needed at the moment were invested. So when the financial meltdown occurred, I lost virtually all my life savings between September 2008 and the end of 2012. Being in fulltime ministry, this was something that was difficult for me to understand, as to why God would allow this to happen. But what God was aware of was that I was depending on Him for everything in my life, except my finances And He of course knew that I would not depend on Him in this area until all my savings were gone. And this was the reason, as He later made me aware of, why He allowed me to lose those funds. He wanted me to learn to depend upon Him totally, knowing that He was more than able to make up anything that I might lose in the financial area!

Now, how this relates to our present subject is that I had a lot of stress in my life at the time as I kept seeing my life-savings dwindle down to almost nothing, and not yet having grasped in God's wisdom why this had all occurred. And as many reading this would know, stress can have, and will often have, a disastrous effect upon one's health. So one night during that time of stress, I woke up in the middle of the night with severe chest pains. I never had a heart attack before, and so had no experience in this area, but this is still the first thought which came to mind, that possibly I was now experiencing one. Now the next step was trying to discern what I should do. Calling an ambulance would have been an expensive proposition, since the cost would be coming out of my own pockets, which were becoming emptier by the day. So I just lay in bed praying, asking God to take the pain away. Finally I came to the point of saying to God that if He wanted to take me at that point, then I was ready to go. So I just put my life into God's hands and just laid there, waiting on God to heal me of whatever was causing the pain. And before long, I just fell asleep.

When I awoke the next morning, I was glad that I was still alive, and also that the pain had gone away. When I knelt for my morning time of prayer with God a few minutes later, He immediately brought the following two verses to mind, verses that I was not personally familiar with at the time, in terms of personal application. But God knew that I had health concerns at the moment and that I had asked him if I was going to die, as part of my prayer to Him the previous night. And now this is what He led His servant to read from His word to encourage and comfort me during this time of stress, first bringing me to Psalm 27:13, where we read, "I would have despaired unless I had believed that I would see the goodness of the Lord in the land of the living," and then to Psalm 56:13, "For You have delivered my soul from death, indeed my feet from stumbling, so that I may walk before God in the light of the living." To say that I was greatly encouraged and relieved at that point would be an understatement! Once again through this experience, God had shown His servant that we can trust Him wholly, even in regards to our health!

So let us begin with one passage, which I have personally been making use of whenever faced with some health condition, that being what God promises us at Philippians 4:6,7, "[6] Be anxious for nothing, but in everything by prayer and supplication with thanksgiving let your requests be made known to God. [7] And the peace of God, which surpasses all comprehension, will guard your hearts and your minds in Christ Jesus." Since God is in control of our health, and since disease or sickness are never a coincidence or a chance occurrence, but are always as allowed of God to serve some purpose of His, then the first thing that God wants us to avoid, when faced with a disease or some sickness, it to give in to anxiety. In other words, God wants us to come to Him in prayer, as we see above, and present our requests to Him, which includes asking for healing, and then we leave the matter with Him. And when we do so, He promises to guard our hearts and our minds in perfect peace until that prayer is answered. I can personally testify to having made use of these verses many times in my life when faced with some health issue.

Another verse that I have used on occasion is what God tells His own at 1 Peter 5:7, "casting all your anxiety on Him, because He cares for you." Here we have the specific reminder from God that He cares for us. After all, we are His very own children yet on earth, as those He has personally saved in order that we might belong to His family eternally. What often also comes to mind at this time, when pondering this, is what God tells us at Romans 8:32, "He who did not spare His own Son, but delivered Him over for us all, how will He not also with Him freely give us all things?" And that includes health! Let us think about this for a moment. Since God gave up His Son unto death on our behalf that there might be the forgiveness of our sins, which are at the root of all disease and sickness, then it follows that God will not hold back from providing healing from disease or sickness for His very own child when requested of Him! So let that be part of our encouragement and comfort in coming to Him for healing!

Let us go on then and note some of God's specific promises for when we, as His children, face some disease or sickness, starting with Deuteronomy 32:39 in part, "See now that I, I am He, and there is no god besides Me; it is I who put to death and give life. I have wounded and it is I who heal," then going on to Jeremiah 30:17 in part, "For I will restore you to health and I will heal you of your wounds,' declares the Lord," and also at Job 5:17,18, "[17] Behold, how happy is the man whom God reproves, so do not despise the discipline of the Almighty. [18] For He inflicts pain, and gives relief; He wounds, and His hands also heal."

Let us also be encouraged and find comfort in what believers have personally prayed, when needing healing from God, noting for instance at Psalm 6:2, "Be gracious to me, O Lord, for I am pining away; heal me, O Lord, for my bones are dismayed," also at Psalm 30:2, "O Lord my God, I cried to You for help, and You healed me," and also at Hosea 6:1,2, "[1] Come, let us return to the Lord. For He has torn us, but He will heal us; He has wounded us, but He will bandage us. [2] He will revive us after two days; He will raise us up on the third day, that we may live before Him."

Then we also need to note that at times God places a condition for His healing, noting for instance what God says at Psalm 41:1-3 in part, "[1] How blessed is he who considers the helpless; The Lord will deliver him in a day of trouble. [2] The Lord will protect him and keep him alive, and he shall be called blessed upon the earth; and do not give him over to the desire of his enemies. [3] The Lord will sustain him upon his sickbed; in his illness, You restore him to health," also at Proverbs 4:20-22, "[20] My son, give attention to my words; incline your ear to my sayings. [21] Do not let them depart from your sight; keep them in the midst of your heart. [22] For they are life to those who find them and health to all their body," and also at Hebrews 12:12,13, "[12] Therefore, strengthen the hands that are weak and the knees that are feeble, [13] and make straight paths for your feet, so that the limb which is lame may not be put out of joint, but rather be healed."

What would also be instructive before we close this chapter is to briefly look at king Hezekiah, as to what he prayed to God when he was sick and told he was about to die, noting what God tells us at 2 Kings 20:1-7, "[1] In those days Hezekiah became mortally ill. And Isaiah the prophet the son of Amoz came to him and said to him, "Thus says the Lord, 'Set your house in order, for you shall die and not live.' " [2] Then he turned his face to the wall and prayed to the Lord, saying, [3] "Remember now, O Lord, I beseech You, how I have walked before You in truth and with a whole heart and have done what is good in Your sight." And Hezekiah wept bitterly. [4] Before Isaiah had gone out of the middle court, the word of the Lord came to him, saying, [5] "Return and say to Hezekiah the leader of My people, 'Thus says the Lord, the God of your father David, "I have heard your prayer, I have seen your tears; behold, I will heal you. On the third day you shall go up to the house of the Lord. [6] I will add fifteen years to your life, and I will deliver you and this city from the hand of the king of Assyria; and I will defend this city for My own sake and for My servant David's sake." ' " [7] Then Isaiah said, "Take a cake of figs." And they took and laid it on the boil, and he recovered."

Here we note that Hezekiah not only received complete healing from God from his mortal illness, when he prayed to God for healing, but we also see that God gave him fifteen additional years. What is interesting to note here is that in those fifteen years Hezekiah's wife had another son, who was to succeed him as king after his death. That king's name was Manasseh, and he became one of the most wicked of kings to ever sit on the royal throne; so wicked in fact that the wickedness of future kings were measured by Manasseh's wickedness! Since this is the only example that we have in all of God's word throughout human history of a person being given an extension on one's life, possibly the lesson to us here is to never ask God for an extension on our life; just for healing!

"Heal me, O Lord, and I will be healed..."

Jeremiah 17:14 in part

CHAPTER FIVE

/ Examining the question of whether God alone has the power to heal today, or is He still giving that power to men?

We have already noted, when looking at Matthew 4:24 in an earlier chapter, that God's Son, The Lord Jesus Christ, had the power of God to heal human beings while on earth at His first coming, further noting here what God tells us at Matthew 9:35, "Jesus was going through all the cities and villages, teaching in their synagogues and proclaiming the gospel of the kingdom, and HEALING EVERY KIND OF DISEASE AND EVERY KIND OF SICKNESS." What is very important to ever remember in regards to God's power to heal human beings is that it is always available, this being true in all ages of time!

And what we also need to be aware of now in this chapter is that this God-given gift to heal was also passed on to the apostles of God's Son, and also other God-selected believers, after He had ascended to Heaven again, after His death, burial, resurrection from the dead, and subsequent ascension. This is clear from what we read of the apostle Peter, for instance at Acts 9:32-34, "[32] Now as Peter was traveling through all those regions, he came down also to the saints (that is, believers) who lived at Lydda. [33] There he found a man named Aeneas, who had been bedridden eight years, for he was paralyzed. [34] Peter said to him, "Aeneas, Jesus Christ heals you; get up and make your bed." Immediately he got up." Here we see that God healed a believer on earth, doing so through the apostle Peter.

And the same was also true of the apostle Paul, who came later, noting what God tells us at Acts 19:11,12, "[11] God was performing extraordinary miracles by the hands of Paul, [12] so that handkerchiefs or aprons were even carried from his body to the sick, and the diseases left them and the evil spirits went out." So we see that this God-given gift to heal was also passed on to the apostles, who gave leadership to the believers in carrying out the ministry on earth, after God's Son has gone back to Heaven again in the ascension. This is also clear from what God tells us at Luke 9:1,2, "[1] And He called the twelve together, and GAVE THEM THE POWER and authority over all the demons and TO HEAL DISEASES. [2] And He sent them out to proclaim the kingdom of God AND TO PERFORM HEALING."

And while all these things are true, the question for us at this point is whether God alone has the power to heal in our day, or is God still seen to be giving that healing power to men today, as He was 2000 years ago? This is a question that I remember being faced with while still just a new believer. I had been invited by a Christian friend to a banquet one evening and what I saw take place there that evening shook me to the core, and not in a good way. What I mean is that God's Holy Spirit in my spirit was giving me so many red flags that my spirit became very distraught and remained so for many days. It was only after God had me do a study of spiritual gifts in His word, including the gift of healing, that I again had peace in my soul in this area. And from that study, which was repeated years later when I was much older in the faith, I discovered some truths about the so-called 'sign gifts,' which led me to conclude that only God heals today and that the 'sign gifs,' which includes the gift of healing, are no longer being given to men today. Let us now go on in the rest of the chapter to learn why that is so.

First then, we are to be aware of the fact that the gift of healing was listed by God at 1 Corinthians 12:8-10 in what has come to be known as the 'sign gifts, adding here verses 4 and 11 for context, "[4] Now there are varieties of gifts, but the same Spirit... [8] For to one is given the word of wisdom through the Spirit, and to another the word of knowledge according to the same Spirit; [9] to another faith by the same Spirit, and to another GIFTS OF HEALING by the one Spirit, [10] and to another the effecting of miracles, and to another prophecy, and to another the distinguishing of spirits, to another various kinds of tongues, and to another the interpretation of tongues. [11] But one and the same Spirit works all these things, distributing to each one individually just as He wills." So the 'sign gifts' are what we read at verses 8 to 10 here. And what would also be useful at this point is to briefly look at the history of these 'sign gifts' among God's people, where we will see that God had a purpose for them, and when that purpose was completed, then these 'sign gifts' ended, which was well before the end of the first century AD!

What is critical to now see and remember is that 'the sign gifts' had their beginning and basis for their existence in the earthly ministry of God's Son, The Lord Jesus Christ, AND LASTED ONLY AS LONG AS THERE WERE APOSTLES ON EARTH! What would be helpful here is looking at what God tells us at Acts 2:22, regarding the ministry of His Son on earth, "Men of Israel, listen to these words: Jesus the Nazarene, a man ATTESTED TO YOU BY GOD WITH MIRACLES AND WONDERS AND SIGNS WHICH GOD PERFORMED THROUGH HIM in your midst, just as you yourselves know..."

And here we have the mention of "miracles and wonders and signs," which God The Father performed through His precious Son, The Lord Jesus Christ, in order to attest Him as truly having been sent from God to those who saw and heard Him in human flesh, after He had started His public ministry. In other words, the miracles, wonders, and signs were merely a means for God to say to mankind, 'stop, take notice of what is being done and said here, for this is My Son, Whom I have sent to earth for you to believe in.'

What has just been said is very important to keep in mind as we continue and now look at the ministry of the apostles, who were being trained on earth by God's Son during the three and half years of His public ministry, and who then gave the leadership in carrying on the ministry on earth, after God's Son had ascended back to Heaven again, as we see take place at Acts 1:9-11. And what is critical to now see is that the same miracles, wonders, and signs which were part of the ministry of God's Son, were now seen to still be in evidence in the ministry of the twelve apostles, and of other apostles which God then raised, such as Paul and Barnabas, and still for the same reason.

In other words, just as God The Father worked miracles, wonders, and signs through His Son while on earth in order to attest to any who came in contact with Him that this was really God's Son in human flesh, sent of The Father under His full authority, and with a message that was from Him to mankind; then now too were the apostles attested to by means of miracles, wonders, and signs, which was God's way of proving that they also had been sent of Him, were under His authority, and were speaking the word of God! And here we can note a very key verse in this regard, which is at 2 Corinthians 12:12, where God says, "The SIGNS OF A TRUE APOSTLE were performed among you with all perseverance, by SIGNS AND WONDERS AND MIRACLES."

And so, once God's Son had returned to Heaven again, the miracles, wonders, and signs were now done by The Father through the twelve at first, and then through other apostles similarly raised of God, such as Paul and Barnabas, and then also through other men, who were believers, during the early days of the church age, such as Stephen and Philip. Both Stephen and Philip were part of the seven men chosen by the believers of the local church at Jerusalem for a special task, as we see at Acts 6:1-5. And please also keep in mind that this is now all during the time of the early church, when The Holy Spirit came from Heaven to indwell the believers of earth to start the third age of time known as 'the church age,' and which was at the time when the letters of the New Testament had not yet been written!

And what should be carefully observed here is that God did not do any more miracles, wonders, and signs in the early church after what He tells us of what He did through the apostle Paul at Acts 19:11,12, which we have already noted, but repeat here again to refresh our memories, "God was performing extraordinary miracles by the hands of Paul, [12] so that handkerchiefs or aprons were even carried from his body to the sick, and the diseases left them and the evil spirits went out." In other words, the 'sign gifts,' which included the gift of healing, were no longer being given to believers after what we read here, which was even before all the apostles had passed from the scene, which was much before the end of the first century AD, and we will now see why!

Take for example the sign gift of prophecy mentioned in the list of sign gifts at 1 Corinthians 12:8-10. Since the letters of the New Testament had not yet been given, then that word from God, which was not yet written down permanently, was being given as a "revelation" from God in the local churches through men known as 'prophets.' When all the letters of the New Testament had been given by God and written down in permanent form, which was well before the end of the first century AD of the church age, there was no more revelation, and the prophets were replaced by the shepherd/teachers, who then taught and exhorted the believers from the written letters or copies made of the letters of the New Testament, when gathered as a local church. There was no longer a requirement for a revelation to be made, or for a prophet to give that revelation.

That is why God tells us at Ephesians 4:11, "And He (God's ascended Son to His church on earth) gave some as apostles, and some as prophets, and some as evangelists, and some as pastors (the Biblical word is 'shepherd') and teachers..." What is critical to see here is that the apostles were now replaced by men who were evangelists, and the prophets were replaced by men who were shepherd/teachers, in each of the local churches on earth, after the letters of the New Testament had all been given by God and written down, which was before the end of the first century AD. What this means for our present purpose here is that the 'sign gifts,' including 'the gift of healing' had ceased to be given to men by then. These sign gifts, which included the gift of healing, were only needed during the foundation stage of the early church, until God's written word to mankind had all been given by God!

Similarly, for example, with two other "sign gifts" mentioned, namely the speaking in tongues and the interpretation of a tongue. Speaking in tongues simply referred to the "sign gift" of being able to speak in an existing known language of the world, that the one speaking it had never learned, so that the supernatural ability to speak it came from God. And an interpretation of a tongue was simply the reverse, in that the speaker, or another person, had the supernatural ability given by God to understand that language and then interpret it for the benefit of the those present in a local church.

And so let us say that we are all gathered as an English speaking local church in Corinth of this time and one in the gathering has the sign gift of being able to speak in the Egyptian language. Since none of us can understand Egyptian, then from the rule God gives at 1 Corinthians 14:28, if there was no interpreter present, then the one who had that supernatural ability to speak in that known language was to remain quiet. However, the interpreter here does not refer to one simply knowing the Egyptian language as something which one had learned, but rather the sign gift of interpretation was being able to understand and interpret in English for the hearers present what the one speaking in Egyptian is saying, without ever having learned the language. To simply interpret because one knows the language through having learned it was not a sign gift. However, to be able to understand the language and interpret it without ever having learned it was indeed a sign gift.

And now that we have a better idea of what some of these sign gifts entailed, then we can note what God led the apostle Paul to write at 1 Corinthians 14:22, regarding the sign gifts of tongues and of prophecy, "So then tongues are for a sign, not to those who believe but to unbelievers; but prophecy_is for a sign, not to unbelievers but to those who believe." Therefore, we see here that God had a purpose in giving the sign gifts, in reference to those mentioned here, and also those mentioned at 1 Corinthians 12:8-10, which was for one to take notice of the one speaking and also of the message being given.

So again, the 'sign gifts,' as were the miracles, wonders, and signs, were designed by God to have people stop and take notice, of what one was saying through a spiritual enablement given by God, as being from God and as being given under His authority. However, as was already mentioned, these sign gifts were no longer required once the letters of the New Testament had been given by God and written down in permanent form, which occurred well before the end of the first century AD.

And before leaving this subject, we certainly need to notice what God also says regarding the sign gifts before He ends 1 Corinthians 12, by saying at verse 31, "But earnestly desire the greater gifts. And I show you a still more excellent way." What God is saying here is that one who is a believer should desire to have the spiritual gifts which have not ceased, and which will last for the duration of the church age, in contrast to the sign gifts, which had just been mentioned at 1 Corinthians 12:8-10, which were temporary in nature. And then when God speaks of showing us "a still more excellent way" at 1 Corinthians 12:31, He is there pointing us to the next chapter, which is 1 Corinthians 13, where God shows that having His Divine love and showing that love to others on a daily basis is worth much more than having temporary sign gifts!

And as an example of this, we only need to notice the first two verses of 1 Corinthians 13, where God compares having His Divine love with the two main sign gifts of prophecy and speaking in tongues in particular, although also mentioning some of the other sign gifts, noting what God there says, "[1] If I speak with the tongues of men and of angels, but do not have love, I have become a noisy gong or a clanging cymbal. [2] If I have the gift of prophecy, and know all mysteries and all knowledge; and if I have all faith, so as to remove mountains, but do not have love, I am nothing."

Therefore, it should be clear to us that God did regard "the sign gifts" as inferior to what was permanent and would last forever, such as the impartation of His love to others, in contrast to what would cease to exist within a few short years, as God makes clear at 1 Corinthians 13:8, "Love never fails;

but if there are gifts of prophecy, they will be done away; if there are tongues, they will cease; if there is knowledge, it will be done away." And please note here that God is saying this in regards to the 'sign gifts!' Therefore the 'sign gifts,' which included the gift of healing, are to be seen as being used by God in the baby stage of the church age, which was until His word to mankind had been fully given in the New Testament portion of God's word, with believers in particular then required by God to live by the permanently given word of God in written form, and no longer rely on sign gifts, which were only meant by God to be temporary.

And as we close this chapter, let us learn a lesson from what God tells us happened one day while His Son was on earth, noting what we read at Mark 5:25-29, "[25] A woman who had had a hemorrhage for twelve years, [26] and had endured much at the hands of many physicians, and had spent all that she had and was not helped at all, but rather had grown worse — [27] after hearing about Jesus, she came up in the crowd behind Him and touched His cloak. [28] For she thought, "If I just touch His garments, I will get well." [29] Immediately the flow of her blood was dried up; and she felt in her body that she was healed of her affliction." This passage was selected to bring out the truth here that only God can heal, and has not given the power of healing even to doctors, seeing from the above example that they did not have the power to heal even while His Son was on earth, and they do not have it in our day either!

"for the kingdom of God is not eating and drinking, but righteousness and peace and joy in the Holy Spirit. For he who in this way serves Christ is acceptable to God and approved by men."

Romans 14:17,18

CHAPTER SIX

/ Looking at some practical examples of what believers can do so as not to hinder God's Hand in keeping us healthy!

The guiding principle that we will use in this chapter is what God tells the human race at Genesis 1:26, "Then God said, "Let Us make man in Our image, according to Our likeness; and LET THEM RULE OVER the fish of the sea and over the birds of the sky and over the cattle and over all the earth, and over every creeping thing that creeps on the earth." What God is seen as doing here is making mankind STEWARDS of all that exists in God's non-human creation. What stewardship means is that mankind has RESPONSIBILITY over God's non-human creation. Let us also be clear here that being a steward means that God is the Owner. We, as human beings on earth, are simply looking after that non-human creation for Him, and will have to answer to Him one day for how we discharged our responsibility as stewards! What this means for each human being personally in time is that we are each responsible to God for what is under our personal care, so that our bodies, the children God may give us, even our pets and the land we own, fall in that category.

And the same is true in regards to our health, for what needs to be grasped here is that we have already seen from 1 Corinthians 6:19,10 that our bodies belong to God, which means that we are ONLY STEWARDS OF THEM and will have to answer to God one day for how we lived while indwelling these bodies, which is just for a time set by God, which of course includes making sure that these bodies remain as healthy as possible while we yet inhabit them!

In the remainder of this chapter then, we want to look at some practical examples, of what we can do as believers to not hinder God's Hand in keeping us healthy. By now, we know that it is God's will not only that we be healthy while we are on earth, but that God is ever working to keep us healthy as His very own children still on earth. And most of the practical examples given here will be drawn from my own life, from before becoming a child of God at salvation and after. This should give us an idea of the responsibility that we have to keep these bodies that God has given us as healthy as possible as stewards of them, for we will have to answer to God one day of how we did!

Before God saved my soul, which just before I turned 30, I had smoked for twenty years and was a heavy drinker. Actually, by the time I was twenty-nine, my liver was such that I was throwing up bile whenever I drank heavily, even sometimes having to go to the hospital because of it. But God did have His servant quit smoking about three months before saving me, when I went to my doctor's office one day for my appointment and read a booklet on second hand smoke while waiting. That scared me so much that I just quit cold-turkey right there and then. The drinking God stopped cold-turkey about three months after I had become a believer. What I learned from these two experiences is that both smoking and drinking, which most often go together, were both detrimental to my health, and if I intended to live for the glory of God in this body of which God had made me a steward, then I would have to give them up and not go back to them.

The next major event relating to my health was not to occur for another 18 years, which was in 1998 and was in regards to the water I was drinking and the food I was eating. By that time, I had been working in our Company's corporate office for the better part of 16 years. One day I found out one of our managers had to retire early due to ill health. As it happened - and I am sure it was no coincidence, for with God there are no coincidences – I made it a point to have coffee with this manager one afternoon, which took up most of the rest of the day, where I asked him what it was that he had that was causing him to leave the Company.

What that man shared that afternoon was to have a dramatic impact on my life, especially after hearing a few months later that this man had already died, which was at a relatively young age. Two of the things which he shared was in regards to the water I was drinking, which was just tap water at the time, plus the food I was eating, which really was whatever I wanted to eat, without any concern whatsoever for whether that food was healthy, in terms of whether it was doing my body any good or not. As a result of that conversation, I began buying bottled reverse osmosis (RO) water from a local distributor and also went to see a naturopathic doctor in regards to what I should be eating. When my wife died near the end of October in 1994, I weighed 176 pounds. Now within a few months of eating healthy, I was down to my normal weight of 140 pounds, which is what I still weigh today. The other thing that I started doing at that time was regular exercise. I bought a used treadmill and got on it every evening after work to relieve stress from my very stressful job.

Little did I know at the time that all these things were to prove extremely helpful, for in early 1999, God called His servant as a non-denominational evangelist and sent me out to my present field of service, very far away from family and friends, where I am still serving Him. And in that time, there have not been any holidays or days off, as I have discharged my ministry seven days a week, God being my witness. So what was implemented just before this fulltime ministry started, such as drinking good water, eating the proper food, and getting adequate exercise was already part of my daily regimen, and served me well in keeping me healthy in God's service!

The other thing that should be mentioned here is getting adequate sleep each night, for in God's original design of us, He meant that our bodies would be repaired while we are sleeping! When I first married my wife, I was living on six hours of sleep a night. Then by the end of 1998, I was requiring eight hours a night in order not to be tired at all during the next day. Then in early 2013, God increased that to nine hours per night as being required so as to not be tired at all during the next day.

What has been mentioned so far are some practical examples of what I do to try to maintain the health I have and so be a good steward of this body, which belongs to God, and also not be hindering His hand in keeping me healthy. One thing I have also been doing for many years, which many readers might also benefit from, is keeping a file of articles that we come across on the internet relating to health. For instance, often the latest studies, relating to such things as cancer and heart health, are not only published in scientific journals, but the gist of the studies is reported in the media. So as a result of reading these articles, I take some supplementation, such vitamin D, fish oil capsules, oil of oregano, curcumin, and drink green tea, as just some examples.

Other things that I do - since part of my ministry is with seniors in a care facility, where all kinds of sicknesses and diseases are generally rampant, due to the nature of these places – is to strip to my waist and wash with an anti-viral soap when I come home, including my head and hair. Then I keep a herbal anti-viral medication for internal use, which I have been using for many years now. Before I started doing this, I was constantly battling infections of every kind as a result of my contact with the seniors. What some people may not realize is that most of the seniors only have a full bath once a week, and sometimes only once every two weeks, depending on circumstances such as whether they were sick on their bath day, or whether the staff was running behind or not.

What has been written here should suffice in giving the reader an idea of the responsibility that we have as believers to do what we can to maintain our health as stewards of these bodies which belong to God, and is apart from what God Himself is doing to keep us healthy as His own children. We only pass through this life once, we might as well be as healthy as possible while we are here!

"And looking at them Jesus said to them, "With people this is impossible, but with God all things are possible."

Matthew 19:26

CHAPTER SEVEN

/ Realizing that God is able to keep believers with the measure of health necessary to complete one's course while on earth!

In this chapter, the intent is on encouraging believers with the realization that God is more than able to keep believers with the measure of health necessary for each one of us to complete our God-determined course while we are on earth! What we need to remember is that God not only saved us (Ephesians 2:8-10), so that we are not only His workmanship, but God is continually at work in our lives to PRESERVE us, which includes our health, from the moment of our salvation in particular, until the day that we are with Him! Let us notice what we read of God at Psalm 36:6 in part, "O Lord, You preserve man and beast," and also at 1 Peter 5:10, "After you have suffered for a little while (as a believer), the God of all grace, who called you to His eternal glory in Christ, will Himself perfect (that is, bring us to spiritual maturity, Hebrews 6:1-3), confirm, strengthen and establish you."

It is only to be expected that since God has a plan for each our lives that He is outworking, and since it is His will that we be healthy as His children while on earth, as we have already seen, then it should not surprise us that God will preserve us, not only alive, but also in health, while He does His intended work in us and through us for which He saved us! Let us reinforce these thoughts with truths from God's own word to us, noting what we read at Isaiah 25:1, "O Lord, You are my God; I will exalt You, I will give thanks to Your name; for You have worked wonders, plans formed long ago, with perfect faithfulness, also at Jeremiah 29:11, "For I know the plans that I have for you,' declares the Lord, 'plans for welfare and not for calamity to give you a future and a hope," and then also noting what God says to His own at Ephesians 2:10, "For we are His workmanship, created in Christ Jesus (speaking of the moment of our salvation) for good works, which God prepared beforehand so that we would walk in them."

God also gives us an actual example from the history of the nation of Israel, in regards to what He did for them in a previous age of time. After bringing upwards of two million people of the nation of Israel out of bondage in Egypt, God led them in the wilderness of Sinai for forty years, until all those of twenty years and above had died, except Joshua and Caleb, before bringing the next generation into the land He promised to give them under Joshua's leadership. Let us notice what God tells that new generation at Deuteronomy 7:14,15, as He is about to have them enter the land He promised to give them, "[14] You shall be blessed above all peoples; there will be no male or female barren among you or among your cattle. [15] The Lord will remove from you all sickness; and He will not put on you any of the harmful diseases of Egypt which you have known, but He will lay them on all who hate you," and also at Nehemiah 9:21, " "Indeed, forty years You provided for them in the wilderness and they were not in want; their clothes did not wear out, nor did their feet swell."

Since it was God's plan for this new generation to be brought to the land of promise, then we see that God not only supernaturally kept them alive, but also kept them healthy until His plan had been accomplished. And we can be sure that what God did for them then, He is also able to do for us now, noting what God tells us at Romans 15:4, "For whatever was written in earlier times was written for our instruction, so that through perseverance and the encouragement of the Scriptures we might have hope," and also at 1 Corinthians 10:11, "Now these things happened to them as an example, and they were written for our instruction, upon whom the ends of the ages have come." Since God has no favorites, then we can be sure that God will do the same for us also, which means we can trust Him to keep us in health until our course through this life as His child as been completed!

As we bring this chapter to a close, one very important truth that we need to be aware of is that the devil, who ever works to prevent us from coming to know God before salvation, continually works after our salvation to try to prevent us from walking in the peace and joy of our new found faith with God! And one of the ways that the devil does this, apart from continually attempting to get us to sin, is to have us continually concerned about our health. I know, for I was on that merry-go-round over six years ago. At first, there was a continual concern over having prostate cancer due to having a higher than normal PSA reading (the PSA test is given to men as the first marker in testing for possible prostate cancer). In fact, at the time my doctor actually told me that he believed that I had prostate cancer, based on the high reading that he was seeing I had.

And so it was not surprising that he did all he could to have me see a urologist for a biopsy. This was something that I was not willing to do, based on what I had read about that procedure, and as a result, the doctor was very angry at me, telling me at the time, "Do not have your family sue me down the road due to refusing to have a biopsy done." What I had also read was that a high PSA was often caused by an enlarged prostate, which was a condition that I knew I had. And as a result of this episode with the doctor, I have not gone back to him in the last six years. But during those six years, the devil tried a new tactic, which was to have me all tied up in knots over heart attacks, due to having chest pains. As a result, I have been to emergency four times during that period to get checked out, being told each time that it was muscle spasms. Twice I was sent to a cardiologist, where further tests were done to confirm that my heart was healthy.

What I have just related here is what I heard a minister in his mid-eighties relate in a sermon I was listening to one day. He too went for many years from the fear of one serious ailment after another, until he too realized the truth of what I have just shared above, in terms of the devil knowing that health is usually a big concern among human beings, and therefore something that he can try to manipulate us with, especially when we are believers. Therefore, it is important as believers that this be a settled thing in our hearts and minds that God indeed desires to not only keep us in health during our stay on earth as His very own children, but God actually will keep us healthy, until we have run our God-given course on earth!

"But food will not commend us to God; we are neither the worse if we do not eat, nor the better if we do eat."

1 Corinthians 8:8

CHAPTER EIGHT

/ Are God's dietary laws, as found in the Old Testament, for today?

As we have read through the Old Testament, probably many times since becoming a believer, we may have noticed that God gave the nation of Israel some dietary laws to follow in the Old Testament, in terms of what foods to eat and what foods not to eat. One passage that clearly sets this out is at Leviticus 11:1-31 for example. We will not quote the whole passage here, but only Leviticus 11:1-10 to give us an idea of what God did allow and what God did not allow the nation of Israel to eat, "[1] The Lord spoke again to Moses and to Aaron, saying to them, [2] "Speak to the sons of Israel, saying, 'These are the creatures which you may eat from all the animals that are on the earth. [3] Whatever divides a hoof, thus making split hoofs, and chews the cud, among the animals, that you may eat. [4] Nevertheless, you are not to eat of these, among those which chew the cud, or among those which divide the hoof: the camel, for though it chews cud, it does not divide the hoof, it is unclean to you. [5] Likewise, the shaphan, for though it chews cud, it does not divide the hoof, it is unclean to you; [6] the rabbit also, for though it chews cud, it does not divide the hoof, it is unclean to you; [7] and the pig, for though it divides the hoof, thus making a split hoof, it does not chew cud, it is unclean to you. [8] You shall not eat of their flesh nor touch their carcasses; they are unclean to you. [9] These you may eat, whatever is in the water: all that have fins and scales, those in the water, in the seas or in the rivers, you may eat. [10] But whatever is in the seas and in the rivers that does not have fins and scales among all the teeming life of the water, and among all the living creatures that are in the water, they are detestable things to you..."

God also gave instructions to the nation of Israel regarding specific parts of an animal that could be eaten and which could not be eaten, noting for instance what God says at Leviticus 7:23-26, "[23] Speak to the sons of Israel, saying, 'You shall not eat any fat from an ox, a sheep or a goat. [24] Also the fat of an animal which dies and the fat of an animal torn by beasts may be put to any other use, but you must certainly not eat it. [25] For whoever eats the fat of the animal from which an offering by fire is offered to the Lord, even the person who eats shall be cut off from his people. [26] You are not to eat any blood, either of bird or animal, in any of your dwellings." And so here we note that the fat and the blood of an ox, a sheep, or a goat were prohibited to be eaten, out of the animals that had been declared clean to eat otherwise.

These two examples should suffice for us to get the picture here, in terms of God prohibiting certain animals and certain foods in the Old Testament. And the question for us now is whether these prohibitions from God, as found in the Old Testament, are still applicable for us today? In providing an answer to that question, we must be aware of the context under which these dietary laws were given. For instance, another way to phrase the Old Testament portion of God's word, the Bible, is as the old covenant, or the first covenant, since the word "testament" also means 'covenant.' What that also means then is that the New Testament portion of God's word is the new covenant, or second covenant.

And in order to see these two covenants mentioned by God in His word, let us note Hebrews 9:15-22 as an example, "[15] For this reason He (God's Son, after He had come to earth in human flesh) is the mediator of a NEW COVENANT, so that, since a death (His own at the cross) has taken place for the redemption of the transgressions that were committed under the FIRST COVENANT, those who have been called may receive the promise of the eternal inheritance. [16] For where a covenant is, there must of necessity be the death of the one who made it. [17] For a covenant is valid only when men are dead (today, we often refer to this as one's last will and testament), for it is never in force while the one who made it lives. [18] Therefore even the FIRST COVENANT was not inaugurated without blood. [19] For when every commandment had been spoken by Moses to all the people according to the Law, he took the blood of the calves and the goats, with water and scarlet wool and hyssop, and sprinkled both the book itself and all the people, [20] saying, "This is the blood of the COVENANT (in reference to the old or first covenant) which God commanded you." [21] And in the same way he sprinkled both the tabernacle and all the vessels of the ministry with the blood. [22] And according to the Law, one may almost say, all things are cleansed with blood, and without shedding of blood there is no forgiveness."

What is critical to observe first from what God is saying here regarding the old and the new covenant is that the old covenant had types, for example, which foreshadowed the coming of God's Son to earth in human flesh under the new covenant. And some of the types were the innocent animals sacrificed, such as oxen, sheep, and goats, which were sacrificed unto death on the altar, as foreshadowing the sacrifice that God's own Son would later make at the cross, where He, as the innocent and sinless Son of God, would give His own innocent and sinless life for a sinful human race.

And so we see from Leviticus 7:25 above that the fat was forbidden to be eaten, because it was reserved for the animal sacrificial system, which foreshadowed the atonement that God's Son would later make on the cross. Similarly, the blood is also seen to have been prohibited from being eaten for exactly the same reason, as we see from what God says at Leviticus 17:10,11, "[10] And any man from the house of Israel, or from the aliens who sojourn among them, who eats any blood, I will set My face against that person who eats blood and will cut him off (meaning that person will be put to death) from among his people. [11] For the life of the flesh is in the blood, and I have given it to you on the altar to make atonement for your souls; for it is the blood by reason of the life that makes atonement."

The atonement that God has in view here, for which the blood, like the fat, was being reserved, is the bringing of two parties, who formerly were separated from one another and not at peace, together as one, this being accomplished through the death of God's own precious Son in the place of guilty sinners at the cross, thereby providing His Father the basis of forgiving sinners who believe in Him! And so God did not want what was for sacred use, the blood and the fat, to also be for common use!

And then the second critical observation that we need to make here, which is why the dietary laws that we noted at Leviticus 11:1-31 were specifically given to the nation of Israel for instance, and not to any other nation on the earth, was due to the fact that during the old covenant, and specifically the second age of it, God was dealing with all the nations of the earth through the nation of Israel. In other words, within the nation of Israel was a small believing remnant which God was going to bring His Son to earth through one day, for one thing; and for another, it was also through this believing remnant within the nation of Israel that God was going to bring His word in written form to all the nations of the earth. What this meant then is that God wanted to set the nation of Israel apart, and specifically the believing remnant within it, because they were being reserved for these special purposes of God! And so the dietary laws were just one example of God's means of setting the nation apart from the other nations of the earth under the old covenant.

But now we need to note that when the new covenant began, this meant that the old covenant system needed to be set aside, since it only pointed to the time of His Son coming to earth, as God made clear to Peter one day, noting what happened at Acts 10:9-16, "[9] On the next day, as they were on their way and approaching the city, Peter went up on the housetop about the sixth hour to pray. [10] But he became hungry and was desiring to eat; but while they were making preparations, he fell into a trance; [11] and he saw the sky opened up, and an object like a great sheet coming down, lowered by four corners to the ground, [12] and there were in it all kinds of four-footed animals and crawling creatures of the

74

earth and birds of the air. [13] A voice came to him, "Get up, Peter, kill and eat!" [14] But Peter said, "By no means, Lord, for I have never eaten anything unholy and unclean." [15] Again a voice came to him a second time, "What God has cleansed, no longer consider unholy." [16] This happened three times, and immediately the object was taken up into the sky."

First, Let us note from this passage that the animals that God showed Peter in his vision were from the list of prohibited animals at Leviticus 11:1-31. Secondly, we note that God tells Peter at verse 13 to go ahead and eat of these previously prohibited animals, but Peter objects, because he was not only of the nation of Israel, but also part of that believing remnant within it, and tells God, "By no means Lord, for I have never eaten any unholy or unclean," that is, from God's prohibited list. But thirdly, let us note what God answers back to Peter at verse 15, "What God has cleansed, no longer consider unholy."

Now the question we need to ask is: Why was the food prohibited under the old covenant suddenly okay for them to eat under the new covenant? And the answer to that question is that Peter was now under the new covenant, no longer under the old covenant, and specifically in the third age of time, which is the first age of the new covenant, where God now had His Son on the earth in human flesh; now dealing with the nations of the earth through the believers of ALL the nations of the earth, and no longer just through the believing remnant of the nation of Israel.

So if one reads what takes place before and after the passage quoted from Acts 10 above, one will see that God was sending Peter to meet with Gentiles, meaning those who were non-Jews, or from among the nations. So before this, those of the nation of Israel, and the believers within it in particular, like Peter, were set apart from the people of other nations and would not interact with them, keeping separate from them, with one means of doing that was through the dietary laws. Now in the present age under the new covenant, God was removing that barrier, so that the nation of Israel was now part of the nations and no longer separate from them. This also meant that there was no longer a distinction in God's sight between Jews and Gentiles in the present age of the new covenant; since under the new covenant, God was dealing with the nations of the earth through all the believers of the nation of the earth! This meant that God's dietary laws to keep the nation of Israel separate from the other nations were no longer required.

And so relating to the dietary laws and whether they apply to us today, meaning in the present age of the new covenant, the answer is 'no,' and hopefully all those reading this will now be able to understand why from the example and explanation provided above. Then just to reinforce the truth that the dietary laws of the old covenant that God gave to the nation of Israel no longer apply to us today, let us note what God's Son said to His disciples one day at Mark 7:14,15,17-23, which we must remember is now after His coming to earth in human flesh, which means it is now during the new covenant, "[14] After He called the crowd to Him again, He began saying to them, "Listen to Me, all of you, and understand: [15] there is nothing outside the man which can defile him if it goes into him; but the things which proceed out of the man are what defile the man... [17] When he had left the crowd and entered the house, His disciples questioned Him about the parable. [18] And He said to them, "Are you so lacking in understanding also? Do you not understand that whatever goes into the man from outside cannot defile him, [19] because it does not go into his heart, but into his stomach, and is eliminated?" (Thus He declared all foods clean.) [20] And He was saying, "That which proceeds out of the man, that is what defiles the man. [21] For from within, out of the heart of men, proceed the evil thoughts, fornications, thefts, murders, adulteries, [22] deeds of coveting and wickedness, as well as deceit, sensuality, envy, slander, pride and foolishness. [23] All these evil things proceed from within and defile the man."

What needs to be observed here is that what we see in brackets at verse 19 is God's comment in His word about what His Son is saying here on earth in terms of ALL FOODS being now clean, that is, being okay for anyone to eat. And so the answer again to the main question relating to this chapter is that in the present age, under the new covenant, there is no food that has been prohibited by God for humans to consume!

"Call to me and I will answer you, and I will tell you great and mighty things, which you did not know."

Jeremiah 33:3

CHAPTER NINE

/ Discerning some health tips from God's word!

After reading the last chapter, there is now one truth which we can bring into this chapter, which relates to our health as human beings, which is that God has placed no prohibition on any food found in nature that we cannot eat! But that of course needs to be understood with some basic discernment. For instance, what God would regard as food that can be eaten would in general be what one grows or what one can find on a farm anywhere in the world; and not necessarily anything and everything that is found in a supermarket or on a restaurant menu! And for obvious reasons!

For one thing, much of the food we have available to us today is so processed as to have all, or almost all, of its nutritional value taken out of it. And this goes all the way from the bread we have available to us, right on to the meat, and includes the milk and eggs also. Then add to this the fact that since the mid-nineties at least, we now have food offered to us that is GMO (Genetically Modified Organisms), that is, that has had its seeds modified in the lab, so that what then comes out of the ground can no longer be considered natural, but is man-made! Therefore, the first health tip that we can take from God's word, based on Mark 7:19 in terms of all foods being now okayed by God to eat, is that what is meant here is what has been grown naturally, without the additions of mankind, such as pesticides, processing, and any genetic modifications! We must remember that in general, the mass production and distribution of food does not have the health of the consumer in mind, but rather more of a concern for the bottom line!

When God told the new generation of the nation of Israel that He was about to give them the land promised to them, which was "a land flowing with milk and honey" (Exodus 3:8), that land was not depleted of beneficial nutrients, so that it did not need fertilizer; nor was it polluted like today, so that the food grown on it did not come with unwanted chemicals; nor was that milk or the honey pasteurized! And what is also important to further observe here is that the milk was not cow's milk, as they had no dairy cows, but rather the milk they drank, and the cheese and butter they made from that milk, came from the goats (see for instance Proverbs 27:27; 1 Corinthians 9:7).

A second health tip that we can discern from God's word is found at John 21:12-15, in what we see take place between God's Son, The Lord Jesus Christ, and seven of His disciples early one morning, "[12]Jesus said to them, "Come and have breakfast." None of the disciples ventured to question Him, "Who are You?" knowing that it was the Lord. [13] Jesus came and took the bread and gave it to them, and the fish likewise. [14] This is now the third time that Jesus was manifested to the disciples, after He was raised from the dead. [15] So when they had finished breakfast, Jesus said to Simon Peter, "Simon, son of John, do you love Me more than these?" He said to Him, "Yes, Lord; You know that I love You." He said to him, "Tend My lambs."

We may all have read this passage of God's word many times and not have noticed the word "breakfast" at verse 12 and 15, as what God's Son Himself invites His disciples to partake of with Him early one morning. Since the life lived by God's Son while on earth was as a Pattern for us to follow (1 Peter 2:21; 1 John 2:6), then we can be sure that breakfast is one meal that God definitely sanctions for us to partake of and not miss! And since we further see God's Son partake of lunch at Luke 11:37 and then also of supper at John 13:3,4, it is clear that God's established pattern for us is to have three meals a day, which should not surprise us as being the pattern even today throughout the world, even among unbelievers. And let us not forget that every single word that God spoke has meaning and is not just filler on a page! Therefore, the words "breakfast," "lunch," and "supper" should be a pattern for us today also!

Another health tip which we can discern from God's word concerns something which has plagued mankind since the dawn of human history on earth, approximately 6,000 years ago, and that is alcohol consumption, which we can also refer to as an intoxicating drink, consisting of wine and liquor. A few years ago, God had His servant do a study of the word 'wine' and associated words in Scripture in order to answer two questions in particular. The first question was whether it was permitted by God for a believer to partake of alcohol; and the second question was whether God's' Son Himself ever partook of alcohol, while He was on earth at His first coming, where He established a Pattern for us to follow? And the answer that was arrived at to both of these questions was that God's Son was never seen partaking of alcohol, that is, of an intoxicating drink, nor did God ever approve of believers, as His own children yet on earth, to partake either!

Another question which arose in the course of the above study was in regards to what can be considered 'intoxicated?' In other words, what was considered intoxicating, and what was considered too much? What was discovered is that in God's word, every mention of the word "wine," whether called simply 'wine,' or 'new wine,' or 'sweet wine,' was in every instance a beverage made from red grapes, which grew on a vine and which was always intoxicating, meaning that from the very first mouthful wine starts to affect one's nervous system, so that the more wine one drinks, the more one comes under it's influence and control.

What this means then is that there is no such thing as non-intoxicating wine in Scripture! And what is also important to keep in mind from the study of wine here is that from the very first mouthful of wine or strong drink, one's nervous system is affected – and modern science confirms this - so that one gradually loses more control of one's self the more one drinks, with being drunk being seen as totally under the influence, that is, under the control of the wine or the strong drink!

The major reasons that God does not approve of believers drinking wine or strong drink is because it is inconsistent with one's profession of having a personal relationship with God through salvation! In other words, a believer is one who is indwelt by The Holy Spirit, so that one is to be under God's control only, as God makes clear to us, for instance, at Ephesians 5:17,18, ""[17] So then do not be foolish, but understand what the will of the Lord is. [18] And do not get drunk with wine, for that is dissipation, but be filled with the Spirit..." Therefore, we see here that God's will for those who are His children yet on earth is to "be filled with The Spirit," and "not get drunk with wine, for that is dissipation," which is the Greek word "Asotia" in the original, and refers to uncontrolled living. And so we see that God wants us under His control, living for His will, as His children, and not as uncontrolled children, living for self, which being drunk with wine characterizes here, which begins even from the first mouthful!

We should not be surprised then to find that the parents of the forerunner to God's Son, that being John the Baptist, were told by God what we read at Luke 1:13-15, "[13] But the angel said to him, "Do not be afraid, Zacharias, for your petition has been heard, and your wife Elizabeth will bear you a son, and you will give him the name John. [14] You will have joy and gladness, and many will rejoice at his birth. [15] For he will be great in the sight of the Lord; and he will drink no wine or liquor, and he will be filled with the Holy Spirit while yet in his mother's womb." In other words, being filled with The precious Holy Spirit is to be seen here as being incompatible with the partaking of an intoxicating beverage, which is true of course for every believer of all ages of time!

And this same message was given to believers by God even in the Old Testament regarding wine and strong drink. For instance, from Leviticus 10:8-11 we see a prohibition under the old covenant for any priest, including the high priest, from drinking wine or strong drink, which were intoxicating, at the tent of meeting. The import for us now is that the high priest then was a picture of the High Priest now, Who is God's Son now in human flesh (Hebrews 3:1), while the priests then was a picture of all believers now (1 Peter 2:9,10)! Additionally, we also note from Numbers 6:1-4 that any believer, man or woman, who wanted to take a vow of separation unto God as a Nazirite, was to totally abstain from wine and strong drink!

The only time God sanctions its use was for medicinal purposes, noting Luke 10:34 and 1 Timothy 5:23, but keeping in mind that in our own day we have many alternatives available to us, even just over the counter, so that there is really no need to resort to alcohol even for this purpose. The point here also is that for a believer to buy intoxicating alcohol, one would have to go to a public place where it is sold, where one could be seen by another person one knows, believer or unbeliever, so that we could be sending the wrong message to others we might be wanting to reach for God, or encourage in the faith!

A final health tip from God's word that we can mention in closing, which should suffice in giving us examples found in God's word for us to use in our own lives, is to note what God tells us at Ezekiel 4:9 in part, "But as for you, take wheat, barley, beans, lentils, millet and spelt, put them in one vessel and make them into bread for yourself..." Let us notice here that God tells His servant the ingredients to use to make bread, and not a specific recipe, in terms of what amount of each to use, which would have to be determined based on the batch size. I remember years ago actually buying bread based on the above, which was called 'EZEKIEL 4:9 BREAD' on the outside wrapper! It was being sold at health food stores and one major retailer that I knew of. I only stopped buying it when I no longer could afford it. But if I ever own a bread maker, I would certainly attempt to make it.

"I am the vine, you are the branches, he who abides in Me and I in him, he bears much fruit, for apart from Me you can do nothing."

Being what God's Son, The Lord Jesus Christ, told His followers at John 15:5

CHAPTER TEN

/ A last word

As we come to the end of the book, there are two things which I would like to share with readers. The first is that my life, the first thirty of it in particular, which was before I came to personally know God, were not easy years, as could no doubt be said for any unbeliever as I then was. But then even after becoming a child of God at the age of thirty, this did not mean that life suddenly became a bed of roses, it only meant that God was now in my life to see me through each day, there to forgive me my sins as I confessed them to Him, and providing me with His life to live by each day, which included keeping me healthy. Within 14 months of my salvation, I had married a widow with three children, ranging in age from 9 to 15. Never having been a husband or a father before, there was a tremendous amount of stress in learning how to live in that new environment.

Less than fourteen years after our marriage – and by this time all three of the children were married – in God's wisdom, He took my wife home. Now within a week of that happening, I was transferred to the new Company's corporate offices, which had bought out our Company during the two months that I was off to care for my wife in the hospital. That meant the stress of losing my wife, compounded by a move to a new Company in a new city, which also meant making new friends and finding a new fellowship to worship with. As one can imagine, the stress from all these sudden changes occurring at once was tremendous, not to forget the stress of starting in a new position!

And this brings me to the second thing which I would like to mention here, which is that in all that time, from my salvation onward, even through all the stressful times, God has seen fit to keep His servant healthy, so that there has never been any serious disease or illness coming upon God's servant so far since the hour and day of my salvation. Those who know me personally say that I look at least ten years younger than my present 66 years. This is all being shared here to not only point out what God has done for His glory, and for which I am really thankful every day, but also to say that what has been written in the book is based on time-tested truth that has been lived out in my own life. And since God has no favorites, what He has done in my life, He is more than able to do in yours also! Praise and thanks be to God is all that I can say in closing!

"For Christ also died for sins once for all, the just for the unjust, so that He might bring us to God, having been put to death in the flesh, but made alive in the spirit…"

1 Peter 3:18

ADDENDUM

/ For those who may not as yet know God

Possibly you have been reading this book and have become aware of not knowing this God Who created us and gave us physical life into this world, and up to now has allowed you to live on earth. However, you do have the desire to know God in a personal way. If this is the case, then this chapter has been written specifically for you. And what God wants you to have in coming to know Him is the peace and joy which comes in knowing that all of your sins committed in your lifetime are forgiven and that you have eternal life with God. And so, your greatest need at the moment is to make peace with God so as to go to Heaven, which is God's eternal home. And so this chapter will help to bring that about by pointing you to God so as to come to faith in Him.

And as we begin, we need to note a most important promise which God makes at Romans 6:23 to all those who do not yet know Him, "For the wages of sin is death, but the free gift of God is eternal life in Christ Jesus our Lord." The good news here is that God offers you eternal life with Him as a free gift, which is to be obtained in His Son, Jesus Christ. What God does not do in this verse from the Bible is tell us how to obtain that eternal life with Him.

Another verse which we can look at where God does let us know how one can obtain that eternal life with Him is noting what God tells us at John 3:16, "For God so loved the world, that He gave His only begotten Son, that whoever believes in Him shall not perish, but have eternal life." Now the added truth which God makes known here is that the eternal life, which He gives to a human being as a free gift, is for those who believe in His Son.

Then the question is: What is it that I am to believe about God's Son, Jesus Christ, which will lead God to give me eternal life with Him forever? And the beauty of God is that He never leaves us guessing, especially when it comes to having a personal relationship with Him, which He desires us to have. Therefore, we should not be surprised when God gives us the answer to our question in what He tells us at 1 Corinthians 15:1-4, "[1] Now I make known to you, brethren, the gospel which I preached to you, which also you received, in which also you stand, [2] by which also you are saved, if you hold fast the word which I preached to you, unless you believed in vain. [3] For I delivered to you as of first importance what I also received, that Christ died for our sins according to the Scriptures, [4] and that He was buried, and that He was raised on the third day according to the Scriptures..." Therefore, "the gospel," which simply means 'good news,' which God wants you to hear and believe in order to "be saved," which simply refers to you coming to know God and have eternal life with Him, is that His Son has already died for you, has already been buried, and has already been raised from the dead again the third day after His death, in order that God would have a basis by which to forgive you of all your sins, which are all against Him, and to freely give you eternal life with Him, for simply believing this message in your heart.

One thing which often prevents a person from believing the gospel at this point is not seeing oneself as a sinner before a Holy God. When we look at ourselves by our own assessment, and especially when we compare ourselves with others around us, we often think of ourselves as being better than others, and so good enough to enter Heaven in our present condition. The problem with this is that it is the product of our own thinking and is not God's assessment of our situation. God's assessment of our situation is as He tells us at Romans 3:10-12,23 in part, "[10] as it is written, "There is none righteous, not even one... [11] there is none who seeks for God [12] all have turned aside... there is none who does good, there is not even one... [23] for all have sinned and fall short of the glory of God..." Quite a different assessment of the human race from that which we as human beings often have of ourselves, is this not? But why would God have such an assessment of the whole human race? For the answer to that question, we need to be aware that God is Creator of all that exists, so that when God created the first man, Adam, at the beginning of time, God created him in innocence, meaning that Adam as first created by God neither knew good nor evil, nor was there any sin anywhere in God's original sinless creation.

However, the day came when God tested Adam with a command, saying to him in the garden of Eden here on earth, which was the perfect environment which God had for him, what we now read at Genesis 2:16,17, "The Lord God commanded the man, saying, "From any tree of the garden you may eat freely; [17] but from the tree of the knowledge of good and evil you shall not eat, for in the day that you eat from it you will surely die." How important to see here that God gave Adam, who although a real person was also representative of the whole human race, the warning of the penalty of death for disobedience to His command.

Unfortunately, the day did come when Adam did partake of the forbidden tree and thereby did sin against God. The moment that happened, Adam not only became a sinner by practice, but also a sinner by nature. One thing my parents had to continually do while under their care was to restrain me from continually going the wrong way, for it seemed that of myself I could not do good, but kept going into sin. The reason this was happening is that from the age of accountability onwards, I had not only become a sinner by practice, but also a sinner by nature. And here the age of accountability needs to be seen as being when as a young child in innocence - which moment is known only by God - one comes to learn the right from the wrong and chooses the wrong, thereby becoming personally accountable to God for one's own sin against Him, since all sin is first of all against Him. And that is why God can say at Romans 3:23 above that "all have sinned and fall short of the glory of God," because God knows that all human beings will go the way of Adam, our representative man, which is also why God can say what He does in regards to the whole of the human race at Romans 5:12, where we read, "Therefore, just as through one man (Adam) sin entered into the world, and death through sin, and so death spread to all men, because all sinned" (from the age of accountability onward).

And so we see that the whole human race is declared by God to not only be sinners by practice and by nature from the age of accountability onwards, but the whole of the human race is now subject to death! In other words, in God's sight the whole of the human race is under the judgment of the penalty of death, due to all being sinners by practice and by nature. You will recall above, in the first verse we quoted from Romans 6:23, God did say there that "the wages of sin is death." And what God means by "death" here is not just loss of physical life, when the physical body we have dies, but also has spiritual death in mind, which is far worse! Spiritual death has its beginning when a separation takes place between a person and God at the moment one becomes a sinner at the age of accountability and ends after the final judgment of time, when God forever casts away from His Presence those who before physical death refused to believe in His Son, Jesus Christ, thereby personally forfeiting the forgiveness of their sins and eternal life with God. And now all such will pay the penalty for their own sins in hell, away from the Presence of God forever.

It is in the midst of such a hopeless situation in which the whole of the human race found itself in that God TOOK THE INITIATIVE and sent His own eternally existing Son into the world, as born of a virgin in the innocence of Adam – so as not to inherit the sinful nature passed on from generation after generation from Adam onwards – so that He might be the acceptable sacrifice offered to God His Father at the cross, there bearing our sins in His body, and there dying the death due our sins! God's Son, Jesus Christ, was then buried and raised from the dead the third day, to ever be alive, for it is through Him, on the basis of what God has done for us through His Son, that God The Father forgives our sins and imparts us eternal life.

Now, by God's grace and His enablement, may you see your need of God's Son to be Your Savior from the penalty due sin, which is death, not only physical, but also spiritual. And by God's grace, may He lead you to believe in His Son, Jesus Christ, and in believing, to receive the forgiveness of your sins and eternal life with Him forever! And based on the truth just shared, the author would now like to ask you a few questions, with the answer being just between yourself and God:

When God says at Romans 3:23, "for all have sinned and fall short of the glory of God," does that include you?

When God says at Romans 5:8, "But God demonstrates His own love toward us, in that while we were yet sinners, Christ died for us," were you included in Christ's death on behalf of sinners?

And when God further says at 1 Peter 3:18 in part, "For Christ also died for sins once for all, the just for the unjust, so that He might bring us to God, having been put to death in the flesh, but made alive in the spirit," were you part of the unjust for whom Christ died?

When God says at Romans 6:23, "For the wages of sin is death, but the free gift of God is eternal life in Christ Jesus our Lord," do you want that eternal life as a free gift from God?

When God says at John 3:16, "For God so loved the world, that He gave His only begotten Son, that whoever believes in Him shall not perish, but have eternal life," do you now believe that Jesus Christ is indeed God's Son in human flesh, Who came from Heaven to this earth to die in your place, so as to save you from ever experiencing the judgment of God leading to an eternal separation from God in hell?

And when God then further says to you at Isaiah 55:6, "Seek the Lord while He may be found; call upon Him while He is near," for His further promise to you here is as we read at Romans 10:9-11,13, "[9] that if you confess with your mouth Jesus as Lord, and believe in your heart that God raised Him from the dead, you will be saved (that is, you will now enter into a personal relationship with God by faith); [10] for with the heart a person believes, resulting in righteousness (that is, in now receiving God's own righteous life to live by), and with the mouth he confesses, resulting in salvation (that is, in now receiving as a free gift the forgiveness of sins and eternal life with God). [11] For the Scripture says, "Whoever believes in Him will not be disappointed…" [13] for "Whoever will call on the name of the Lord will be saved." Will you now call upon God from your heart, telling God in your own words your answer to each question that has just been asked?

The author's prayer for you at this point, as you now call upon God by His grace, is what we read at Romans 15:13, "Now may the God of hope fill you with all joy and peace in believing, so that you will abound in hope by the power of the Holy Spirit."

If there is anyone who desires further spiritual help, please visit my website below:

http://servantofmosthigh.com

To God alone be all praise, honor, and glory, with thanksgiving, both now and forevermore! Amen, amen, and amen.

/ The next book

The next book that God has given His approval to, and for which He also supplied the title, is "Love Is More Than A Four Letter Word!" This will be a love story and is the seventh book in the Christian Fiction Library series. But in case it is not the book that will be written, readers may want to stay current with the author's website below, under "Life Enhancing Books," or under "What's New," where it will be made known if another book has been written. My main website is:

http://www.pilgrimpathwaypublications.com

And if you have enjoyed reading this book or any other of the author's books, please feel free to give me feedback at the above website; and also let family, friends, and co-workers know about this book and other books. The author is not on any social media sites, so he relies on God and readers like you to spread the word. May God bless you for doing so!

www.ingramcontent.com/pod-product-compliance
Lightning Source LLC
Chambersburg PA
CBHW050412290526
45786CB00003B/1226